CROWDBREAKERS

BOB MOFFETT

Illustrated by SIMON JENKINS

Pickering Paperbacks

Dedicated to Jill

© Bob Moffett 1983
First published 1983 by
Pickering & Inglis Ltd.,
3 Beggarwood Lane, Basingstoke, Hants RG23 7LP

ISBN: 0 7208 0513 9

Phototypeset by Input Typesetting Ltd, London SW19 8DR
Printed and bound in Great Britain at
The Camelot Press Ltd, Southampton

Contents

Preface

I was asked by the Spring Harvest committee in 1979 to give a series of seminars on the subject of evangelism and methods of communication. I went through the process of researching my subject and prepared my overhead transparencies ready to speak to what I had estimated would be about thirty people. On the morning of the seminar that I was sharing with a colleague and a friend, over ten times my original figure turned up to see, in the words of now another friend, 'a garden gnome in action'. During the afternoons we also discovered to our dismay that we were attracting approximately 200 youth leaders to a session on 'ideas' for youth groups. Attempting to analyse the reasons for such a growing interest in youth work has led me to write this book. It became an ever increasing conviction from God that I should write down what I had learned through many painful experiences and episodes of youth leadership, so that others may not make *my* mistakes.

I hope that you will be stimulated as you read 'Part One' of this book, and use 'Part Two' as resource material. I am aware that this work may also cause some more experienced youth workers to disagree with some of the material; for this I must apologise in advance and ask you please to correspond so that we may grow in understanding together.

I would like to acknowledge my gratitude to Y.F.C. in the United States and F.Y.T. of Australia for their kindness in allowing me to view and use some of their 'games'.

I am very grateful to a number of people who have laboriously typed my early draft manuscripts: Lynn, Alice and Karen. A particular thank-you goes to my wife Jill who has not only typed the final draft but has assisted me in her devotion and dedication to the hope that is within us: 'With God . . . a mind to work.'

One final thank you must go to all those who have, fortunately, unfortunately, come my way, and received at my hand (and their expense) the products of such activities: messy hair; shaving foam; stomach aches for days; felt tipped feet . . . AND NO FRIENDS!!

Bob Moffett

PART ONE

1 The Role of the
Christian Youth Leader

I will assume that you are fully aware of the basic spiritual requirements of the 'ideal' Christian youth leader: a person of prayer and knowledge of the Bible; full of concern and compassion; someone who can lead by example, etc. With these qualities in mind here are a few practical thoughts in regard to the role and responsibilities of the leader as you prepare your programme and run your group.

The Leader:
1 *must work out his goal or objective* for the group and communicate these to his colleagues (see section titled 'Programme Planning').
2 *has the total responsibility* for everything that occurs under his jurisdiction, i.e. 'the buck stops here'.
3 must be *imaginative and enterprising* with ideas and/or draw creative thinking from others (see section on 'Brainstorming').
4 must *clearly define the areas of responsibility* of each of his helpers in their respective activities and assist them to achieve realistic goals.
5 will *direct training* where necessary; this does not mean that he will actually do the training, but will make it available.
6 will *support, encourage and back* his assistants even though there may be an element of doubt in an action or decision that has been made – particularly in the case of disciplinary action.

7 is responsible for the *co-ordination of the programme* and must be fully aware of this in case of an emergency so that he can act in a calm responsible way at all times.

The Leader CANNOT:
1 lose his temper or raise his voice in anger.
2 panic, but act confidently at all times even though the roof if falling in!
3 leave the club or premises without advising his helpers and getting their agreement.

The Leader MUST ALWAYS BE AVAILABLE.

One of the essential qualities of youth leadership is that you are constantly looking around for potential leadership among the senior young people. I have a strong belief that we should be constantly testing the potential in the responsibilities that we give.

As most youth leaders are usually at least one generation older than the young people who are members, it is sometimes a healthy idea to have some form of committee to assist in organising the programme. However, I rarely call any group of this nature a 'committee' as this suggests 'power' to control. I tend to call these 'working groups' or 'action groups' which give a strong indication that the young people are in that position to 'do' rather than to 'sit'.

If you look at the diagram graph below this may help you to work out where you are on this graph and whether it is the best position for you to be in your particular situation.

Diagram after Warren G. Schmidt

Position A TELLS. The leader decides, then announces his decision. This is usually someone who is just starting up a programme and needs to exercise authority at the outset by presenting working programmes to enable the youth to do at least something in the first few weeks even though it may be experimental.

Position B SELLS. The leader decides, then tries to 'sell' his decision to the youth even though his mind is already made up and will not be changed. This at least is a better position than 'A' as the decisions will probably (hopefully) sound more convincing even though it may be *fait accompli*.

Position C TESTS. The leader presents a tentative decision to the Group and asks advice before making a definite decision.

Position D CONSULTS. The leader presents the problem or situation to the group and seeks advice *before* making his final decision. Like position 'C' this is generally a very good position to be in, as invariably young people will still find it difficult to make decisions although they like to feel they have been involved in the decision-making process.

Position E JOINS. The leader asks the group to decide, attempting to give guidelines and a framework of limits in which decisions can be made. A word of caution here – if you allow the group to make decisions, and then if you ever have to veto such a decision, your position of trust is seriously undermined.

What is the best position for a youth or church leader? Somewhere between B, C and D. Either end will invariably cause problems. However, each group is different, so it is not where you are on the scale that is important so much as THAT YOU KNOW WHERE YOU ARE.

Finally, just a pertinent comment to close this section: if you don't know where you are going as a leader then why expect much more of those who are following?

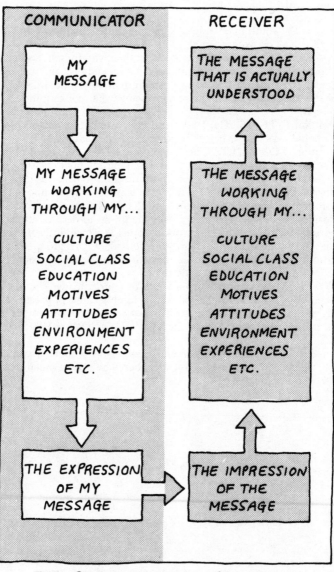

THE COMMUNICATION PROCESS

2 ' 'Ere, what ya say?'

We are all in the world of communicating and as youth workers our problem is even more acute. Not only are we trying to bridge perhaps at least one generation gap, but we are probably trying to communicate on a level that is not easily understood, by the young people in our charge. In this chapter, which I see as the crux of the whole book, I will attempt to define some of the real problems in attempting to communicate a simple message to someone in your youth group. If you don't face up to these problems then you're going to have to take the rough road of mistake after mistake, casualty after casualty, I did.

Start by looking at a model on 'communication'. Keep one eye on the diagram (p. 8) and the other on the reading matter, and follow this discussion through. If I have a 'message', for example 'Jesus is my Saviour', this relatively simple message needs to be communicated through my culture, social class, education, motives, attitudes, environment, experience, etc.

In all of these areas I have consciously or unconsciously made assumptions about my own understanding of what is in my mind when I say 'Jesus is my Saviour'. In other words I think I understand what I mean when I communicate my message. As you are probably aware, the teenage years are ones in which issues are seen in terms of 'black and white'. It is only as you grow older that you realise there are 'grey' areas to particular subjects. As you attempt to communicate to teen-agers you will be aware that your modus operandi will be completely different from that of the 'receiver' of your message.

Returning then to my message 'Jesus is my Saviour', I must now attempt to 'express' it to the receiver. This may be done verbally, by action, by sight, or by any other of our five senses. The message in the mind is no good to the 'receiver' unless it can be expressed in some form. Moving on now to the 'receiver' . . . what does he see or hear . . . what is the impression received. Naturally this is going to be coloured by the culture, social class, education, motives, attitudes, environment, experience, etc., of the receiver.

If these characteristics are similar to those of the 'communicator' then the greater the chances of effective communication. Finally, in the process, 'What is actually understood' in the mind of the receiver is often different from the message in the mind of the 'communicator'. May I give you a couple of examples – 'Jesus is my Saviour' became 'Jesus smells' in the mind of a fourteen year old boy. How? 'Saviour' in his mind was a word that he did not really know and so he turned it into the word 'savour'. He knew the word had something to do with smell, so the message he understood was that Jesus smells.

Without boring you with too many examples (we could probably put together another book on such an exercise) I will give you one more passed on to me by a musician friend who asked a group of twelve year olds the whereabouts in the Bible of Adam and Eve. The response was spontaneous and enthusiastic: 'The book of Guinness!' What then are the implications for us in the area of youth work (or any other form of ministry)?

1 *Communication by its very nature demands a reaction*

So much of our communication these days is done from a distance. Someone speaks and we listen. The days are gone when we can expect people to fill the pews to hear a great or less famous preacher sock it to them. In an age when our educational system teaches young people to ask questions, we can no longer expect these young people to listen to what we have to say, without allowing them to 'react'. Sometimes when I preach in churches, I ask the congregation to react, by requesting anonymous questions written on pieces of paper which I have provided prior to the service. We then have a second 'offering' to collect the questions, and I attempt to give honest answers to genuine questions. From time to time with young people I ask them to do exactly the same thing, but I take it a stage further, and ask them just to 'react' to the whole of the evening's programme. The only proviso that I make is that they must be totally honest, and if they are going to prefix their comments with 'I think it was rubbish' or 'I thought it was great' they must give their reasons. Naturally if they want to discuss things further then they can also indicate this on their reaction card. If you are going to use this system to check your communication then be ready for a shock. I have received extremes of comments at both ends of the spectrum in language that I would prefer not to use myself! If you want to use 'reaction cards' on a regular basis I would suggest the following as a basic format – keep it simple.

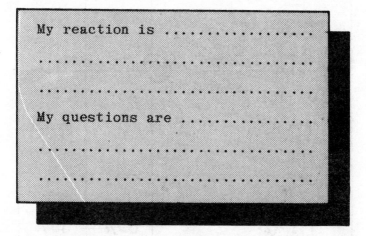

My reaction is ....

....

....

My questions are ....

....

....

If you are going to leave space for questions, then either you tackle them on the next meeting or you ask those who wish to do so to put their names at the bottom of the card. Never ask questions that demand a 'yes' or 'no' answer as that is all you will get – and that is no real check on your communication.

2 *Christian communication should be enthusiastic*
Enthusiasm derives from the Greek, meaning 'inspired by God'. Whether our subject is heavy or light there must be a real conviction of belief in its expression.

3 *Effective communication must be visual and active*
A couple of years ago I uncovered the following information (shown on chart) in a missionary magazine. It upheld a conviction that I have had for a number of years that verbal communication is narrow and limited. As we look at Jesus' teaching approach this becomes obvious, but that will be seen in a later session.
Unfortunately the missionary organisation was unable to substantiate their figures, so I am not offering these as conclusive proof of what I am about to conclude. If, however, these figures are correct, of which I have very little doubt, then I can fully understand why television is such a powerful communicator. It is hitting at two of our

11

MESSAGE RECEIVED BY	INFORMATION REMEMBERED AFTER	
	3 HOURS	3 DAYS
HEARING	70%	10%
SEEING	72%	20%
HEARING AND SEEING	85%	65%

most powerful senses. A youth leader then who is really wanting to communicate effectively must be very visual in his approach – the use of audio-visuals becomes imperative as a prerequisite for imparting even the most basic of information. Jesus did this in the minds of his listeners. Even if he were not pointing to a particular object, he stimulated the minds of his listeners by using pictorial examples: sheep, branches, light and darkness, bread, salt, etc.

4 *Communication in the Old Testament*

a *The Religious Historical Stories*
In the books of Ruth, Jonah, Esther and Songs of Songs (or Song of Solomon), we find historical stories entertaining in themselves and yet containing, at the same time, deep spiritual truth about the covenant grace of God.
Consider the drama of Jonah in the great fish; the beautiful romance between Ruth and Boaz; the collection of love poems and

songs between a man and a woman in the Song of Solomon, and the intriguing account of Esther and Mordecai as they planned to save the Jews from extermination.

b The Psalms
In the Psalms we have the most famous poetry in the world. Written by a number of poets expressing utmost despair on the one hand and the glorious majesty of God at the other end of the spectrum.

c The visual Symbols
Let us look at just one example of dramatic symbolism in the Old Testament. *Jeremiah* demonstrated God's message to his people through very explicit visual aids:

. . . the linen shorts and the wine jars (Jer. 13)
. . . the iron pen (Jer. 17)
. . . the potter and his clay (Jer. 18)
. . . the smashed clay jar (Jer. 19)
. . . the wooden and iron yoke (Jer. 27 and 28)
. . . the buying of the field at Anathoth (Jer. 32)

The vivid demonstration of God's word through drama was very much a part of the message of God.

5 Communication of the New Testament – Jesus, communicator-par excellence
Jesus attracted the people not only because he performed incredible miracles but also because of his communicating power. He was always using parables, drama, picture and object lessons, epitomising this through his death on the cross expressing his love for mankind.

Notice a number of aspects to Jesus' approach:

a *Jesus was authoritative.* He had understanding, depth and background information (historical and biblical) (Matt. 12:38–42).

b *Jesus was visual.* He used objects and pictures that were familiar to the people (Luke 21:29–32; Mark 4:21–23).

c *Jesus was simple.* Making in-depth statements in easily understandable manner, eg speeches on Light, Bread, Good Shepherd, The Vine (John 6:35; 8:12; 15:1).

d *Jesus did not always give answers.* He expressed many of his teachings in parables so that: ' . . . they look, but *do not see,* and they listen but *do not hear* or understand' (Matt. 13:13). We must not always express the whole counsel of God: we must trust the Holy Spirit more to give them understanding.

e *Jesus was interesting.* Latin Saying 'Veritas plateat, veritas placeat, veritas moveat' (Make truth plain, make truth interesting, make truth moving).

f *Jesus used humour*. Examples: The joke about the speck and plank in your own eye (Matt. 7:3–5). Forgiving someone 490 times (Matt. 18:21–22).

g *Jesus used poetry*. Consider the freshness of the message of the Beatitudes (Matt. 5).

h *Jesus used argument*. Jesus was not afraid of debating and arguing his case with others, eg. Sabbath (Matt. 12:22–32).

Jesus communicated the 'good news' through a variety of styles and methods, each one of them sensitive to the needs of the particular community and individuals he was addressing.

The Communication of Paul:

a *Notice the varying styles of Paul* in his writings to the churches, eg. compare Romans with Corinthians, or Philemon with Galatians, or Timothy with Ephesians. Paul used different approaches to different situations.

b *Paul's preaching* varied between races and countries, eg compare Paul's sermon in the synagogue at Antioch (Acts 14) and his preaching to the Athenians (Acts 17). It is important to note that Paul quoted their own poets, Epimenides the Cretan and Aratus a Cilician. Paul spoke the language within the culture . . . 'So I become all things to all men, that I may save some of them by whatever means are possible! Paul's intention was not to express a logical watertight system, but to use all possible means of declaring the message of the Jesus, crucified, buried, resurrected and glorified.

6 *The Place of the Holy Spirit in our communicating*

Without fervent prayer and belief in the Holy Spirit to convict and convince, then all our efforts to communciate are worthless. However, I would refute the idea that because we are relying on the Holy Spirit we do not need to prepare our youth activities. Sometimes God does give us a message on the spur of the moment but generally God gives fruit from our hard work and study. Poor preparation leads to rigidity and inflexibility in a poor process of communication of the most boring kind. I think too many of us are well aware of the results of this in our youth programmes.

Finally, to summarise this section, I quote a Youth For Christ publication, which although primarily about evangelism is very relevant to communication. 'We should not be afraid of rejection; if rejection equals failure then Jesus failed many times; ultimate failure in evangelism is when we don't give folk anything to reject.'

3 Programme Planning

It would not be necessary to do much research to find out what is the question most often asked by youth leaders. It is the question that I have been asked by so many of the thousands of youth leaders I have spoken to over the years. It does not matter to what country you go, what the age group is or how large the group may be. The question: WHAT CAN I DO . . . next week? Working out fresh new imaginative and exciting ideas each week causes more anxiety and frustration than probably any other problem for the average youth leader.

The real problem, however, is that many youth leaders do not know where they *are* going – they do not have specific goals to aim at and therefore succeed at scoring misses most of the time. The second problem is that many youth leaders find it difficult to plan. They might have good ideas, or even goals to reach or aim at, but they cannot plan in such a way that the activities become operational. Another problem is that one can never pick up the good programme ideas when you want them.

In this section I will try to give help in these three areas . . . they are only theory until they are put into practise . . . you can only say (as I have done many times) 'It won't work', until you have tried it.

Goal Scoring
I am indebted to my reading of Engstrom and Dayton's books on

management for this and the next heading. They opened my eyes to a whole new dimension of understanding. Like so much church work we often fail in our mission because we do not really understand what we are trying to achieve. We may talk about 'winning Glasgow for Christ', 'running an effective church' or 'having a successful youth work', but all of these have a very little meaning. Although we can understand them in general terms they are too vague for us to really effectively act upon them. Goals are important to help us out of the 'verbal fog'. What do we mean then by 'setting goals'. According to one definition of the Oxford English Dictionary, a goal is 'the object to which effort or ambition is directed; the destination of a journey'. For us to set a goal or goals means an effort directed in a particular way to bring into being a situation that we feel is important to maintain or to change. Why are goals so important? They help us in the following ways:

Spiritually, goals are statements of faith (compare Phil. 3:13,14). We are saying before God in prayer that this is what we believe God wants us to achieve in the future and that we trust in him to help us fulfil such a goal.

Psychologically, they provide signposts along the road giving us direction. It takes the emphasis off the negative and the problems that you face and directs it towards the positive . . . the potential situation.

Socially, goals are important because we can share them. If you do not know what you are trying to achieve then it is more than a little difficult sharing the 'nothing' with others and expect them to get excited.

Physically, goals help us to sort out the demands upon our time. In other words they save us chasing our tails doing everything and feeling that we have done nothing. If we are specific in our goals then our energy is only expended in that one direction.

Seven Steps to Setting Goals

1 Understand your goal – what is it that you actually want to happen?
2 Picture the situation – what would it be like?
3 State some 'long-term' goals – what steps would lead to the situation in '2'.
4 State your 'immediate' goals – what should you do now?
5 *Act* – do it!
6 Behave as if your goals are working – accept the fact goals are statements of faith and believe in your careful and prayerful action. Come out with confidence that what you have stated is going to happen.
7 *Keep praying*

Take as an example only a youth leader who says, 'I want to be known as an effective youth leader.' As we have said, this is too vague to really mean very much; so let us use this example to set out what goals one may introduce to bring about the overall purpose. It is important to note that when you set 'goals' they must be measurable in time and space – see example.

Example

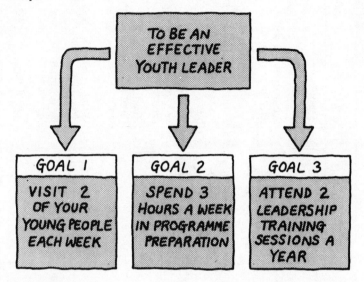

Planning Success:

Now that you have set your specific measurable goals how do you make a plan to achieve them? Take a blank piece of paper and draw a diagram similar to the one titled 'Planning with Goals' (p. 18). Put in the heading titles and columns numbers and proceed as below:

Column 1 *My Goal*: Identify your goals and write them in.
Column 2 *Present situation*: Describe your current situation making sure that it is an honest appraisal.
Column 3 *Forces Helping*: List those forces that are assisting you in your situation. Don't be modest. State what you are good at.
Column 4 *Forces Hindering*: List those forces that are hindering you in your situation – usually this tends to be longer than '3'.
Column 5 *Steps to Goal*: Prepare a list of specific measurable steps towards that goal.

After this ask yourself these three questions:

Is is practical?
Is it realistic?
Do I have to replan? Planning is one of those activities that many of us tend to leave to another day, but this is merely cutting our feet from under us when we do so. Here are a few hints to explain the 'whys' of planning:

Planning by definition is trying to discover how to accomplish our goals.

1 My Goal	2 Present Situation	3 'Forces' Helping	4 'Forces' Hindering	5 Steps to Goal
Visit two young people a week	Visit no one at present	Three nights a week are free. Acceptance by the youth as their leader.	Responsibilities towards the family. Doing things twice a week already. When can I prepare?	Tuesday will be visiting. Wednesday – I will telephone them to arrange the visit.
Spend three hours a week in programme preparation	Spend 1½ hours in preparation.	I do really have more time. My family are sympathetic and involved in the club.	Not sure how to prepare properly. The other leaders may feel that I am being too organised.	Thursday – preparation between 19.00–22.00 hrs. See Bill for advice – he's good on preparation. Read a book every three months on youth work.
Attend youth-leadership training sessions twice a year	None, although I went to one a few years ago.	I can afford two Saturdays a year. I am keen to be trained – I think.	Where do I find suitable training at my level?	Write to Y.F.C. for advice. Be prepared to 'travel' for training courses. Encourage colleagues.

Planning saves times in the long run.
Planning is moving from the NOW to the THEN and FROM the potential to the possibility.

Plans, like goals, are statements of faith.
Plans have the potential for flexibility and adaptability which gives us a certain amount of freedom and liberty in our programmes. Bad planning, however, or a complete lack of it tends towards rigidity and restriction.
Planning helps us to communicate our intentions to others as well as to ourselves.
Better to fail on paper than in practice with people.

Brainstorming
A relatively new concept in this country, this is an exciting way of bringing together numerous ideas in a short time. The advantages are that you are able to bring a fresh point of view to age-old problems, provide a means of achieving your planned goals, and create an enthusiasm for using the same old perennials.

How to Brainstorm:
1 Choose a specific problem or subject that you wish discussed. Like goals they should not be of a general nature, they should be quite definite, eg. What kind of programme evening would be the most effective for our 'first night' of the autumn term?
2 Arrange for a few interested colleagues and senior youth members to attend an informal get together. Explain the subject problem and the concept of brainstorming in advance.
3 When your 'brainstormers' arrive provide a relaxed atmosphere to loosen them up.
4 State the rules for brainstorming. You have a set time (eg, 2 minutes) to throw out as many ideas as possible about the subject given. These should be quick phrases and as crazy as they wish.
   There is to be no criticism eg, 'We've tried that before'.
   Quantity at this stage is better than quality.
5 Organise a 'secretary' and a 'timekeeper'.
6 At the end of the session, the group carefully works through the suggestions, taming the outrageous, adapting the potentials and screening the impossible to produce the required results.

Let me give you an example of a brainstorming session on the subject:

'What to do on a Saturday afternoon in summer'. The group consisted of a number of youth leaders who were being trained in a variety of skills, including 'brainstorming'. By the time we reached this subject they were relaxed and feeling in the mood for almost anything. Therefore it was not surprising that out of the list there were three really zany ideas that took my fancy: granny bashing, chariot racing and crocodile fighting. Putting these three together it became obvious that what we had here was a brilliant idea for a Saturday afternoon activity. a sponsored granny chariot race, ie, youngsters dressed up as grannies pushed along in wheelchairs (wheelbarrows or similar) by a relay team bashing each other with old (crocodile) handbags. What a sight . . . what publicity . . . what a thing to talk about on Monday at school!

Recently my name appeared on 'Swap Shop' on BBC 1 for spaghetti knitting – an idea that came out of a brainstorming session.

In your programming *think big! think dangerously!* and you may just be in step with the young people. If they think your idea is stupid then DO IT. If they say they don't want to do it, cajole them into it with all the zeal and enthusiasm you can muster and I can almost guarantee that they will love it. The proof – they moan about it for months!

4 The Room

'The blank sparsely painted walls stare ominously through the dimly lit uncomfortable rooms where people sit mysteriously on upright chairs talking uneasily one to another in deep volcanic tones.'

Are these the first lines from the latest spy thriller . . . or some secret coded plot of James Bond? If it only were! The truth, I am afraid, is that it is the description of an average youth gathering, meeting in the sacredness of – yes you have guessed – the CHURCH HALL.

So where should we hold our youth meeting? The answer very simply is in the best place – and that is where the young people in your charge feel the most comfortable and the less inhibiting for the programme you have arranged. To hold a discussion for five or six in the average church hall is not only stifling but also demoralising for lively energetic interaction.

From my experience using someone's home for youth activities can be very rewarding. Particularly if it is the home of the youth leader as it will consequently lead onto visits of your group at other times during the week. A truly sincere leader will naturally find this an excellent way of 'keeping in touch'. However, one word of caution: to keep your sanity as a leader (and that also of the family) you will need to specify which particular nights your house is open for unscheduled visitors!

Here are a few practical suggestions – a check list on small but important details that may help your programme to run smoothly:

a If you have a discussion *chairs* should be positioned so that everyone can see each other. Preferably these should be comfortable and old! They must be facing away from the door so that anyone coming in late does not distract the whole group.

b Lighting should be adequate but not brilliant. Careful lighting may assist some of your less vocal members to be a little less embarrassed about participating

c *Ventilation* and *heating* are most important features in keeping (yawn) maximum (yawn) attention (yawn). It is preferable to keep the heat temperature slightly lower than comfortable to allow for raised tempers and heated discussion.

d If you are serving *refreshments*, keep them simple and basic. This not only saves time but also allows you to go to almost any youth member's house for your meetings without embarrassment to any individual.

e Take necessary precautions to *protect furniture, carpets, curtains*, etc. Particularly if you are going to use many messy crowdbreakers in this book. Take it as a rule of thumb, if you leave just a square centimetre of unprotected carpet that is just where the messy object or liquid is going to drop. Remove all valuable items from the room; not because you do not trust the young folk but it saves uneasy feelings on both sides if the Ming vase falls into a million pieces because somebody breathed too hard in the wrong direction.

f Whether you are in a church hall or home, remember there may be *neighbours* either side of the building who may not want to participate in your programme!

g If you are using a church hall, then *limit your activities* to the rooms that you or your colleagues can directly supervise – this includes the toilets.

h *Cram* as many young people into a room as it will comfortably hold. Naturally this will alter to fit the activity. However, as another general rule: a crowd attracts a crowd – even if there are only three. Simply expand the area of operation as the numbers increase. This gives the impression that there is always a crowd and that it is possible to just fit another person into such a popular event. Don't be tempted as numbers increase to jump from a large room to a big hall. What was a crowded cosy group in the relaxed atmosphere of a 'lounge' may feel totally 'at sea' in the spaciousness of even the most comfortable church premises. A final comment about 'the Room' is this, if you want the young people to respect the premises then whatever the decor, style or furnishings keep it reasonably tidy. Sound 'room' planning can give 'room' to manoeuvre in the long run.

PART TWO

5 Crowdbreakers

They drift in 5, 10, 15 even 30 minutes late each week, eleven of them looking as if they expect this to be their last hour on earth. Collapsing on the nearest chairs they tense themselves for the painful inevitable drone of the monotonous dulcet tones of the youth leader as he attempts to 'sock it' to them again. After the set hour which has included at least ten minutes of silent answers to the questions they cannot remember even hearing, they saunter off, glad that once again they have survived another mind boggling . . . exciting . . . yawn . . . energising . . . yawn . . . evening at the . . . yawn . . . church's weekly youth event.

It's twenty minutes before the official opening time and already the place is full of coffee and Cola drinking teenagers larking and laughing about . . . swopping stories of the weekend's youth activities; a real snowball fight in the middle of summer. 'How on earth did they do it?' asks Pete of Susan, talking about John and Sandra the youth leaders. 'They really fooled us . . . a lorry full of the stuff from the local icecream manufacturers; my mates at school thought I was lying. Some may even come tonight 'cos they can't believe some of the things we get up to.' Suddenly a voice, amplified by a hidden P.A. system, booms out and slowly states that 'tonight we are going to look at 'DEATH . . . DEATH – THE GREAT MYSTERY''.' John (the youth leader), whose unmistakable voice had emitted the words, is already in the

23

middle of the group before the taped message has ended. He is explaining that Sandra has taken her cassette recorder out to the shopping centre the day before and recorded people's response to 'What will happen to you when you die?' Three minutes later Sandra is organising one of the first out of three Crowdbreakers that evening on the subject of DEATH . . . but suddenly, as the third game is at its climax, all the lights go out . . . there are blue and white flashes as a gun is fired into the room. The lights go on again as suddenly as they had gone off and John is found standing in the middle of the room with a starting pistol in his hand as Pete, Susan and others try to convince him that they knew all the time it wasn't real.

John and Sandra pass out pens and cards and ask for 'honest' anonymous reactions to the incident before proceeding with an in-depth discussion and Bible study on the subject.

After the 75 minutes they had allowed for his session John and Sandra 'wrap up' the evening with the young people wanting to go on and learn more. However Sandra ignores their request, passes out further biblical references on the subject of death to pacify them and announces the title of next week's programme: 'Jesus Christ, liar, lunatic or Lord?'

Two scenarios with the same youth leaders and young people but a completely different approach to the programme. I believe very strongly that learning should be fun, even if at times the learning turns out to be a painful experience. This section then is on the use of Crowdbreakers as *part* of your totally exciting programme.

6 Crowdbreakers and You

Crowdbreakers are no substitute for a well organised and prayerfully planned programme. They are to enhance your existing programme by adding an element of participation and involvement in the subject you have chosen for that particular evening.

As leader, you are probably the keypin as to whether or not your programme will be successful. Your relationship with God and your enthusiasm with the teenagers are most important and you must never rely on methods alone. If, however, you are going to use Crowdbreakers then please bear in mind the following:

The Leader and Crowdbreakers

1 Unless you express fervently your zeal for such an approach forget it! Using games as an integrated part of your teaching programme requires a balanced attitude from the leader.

2 You must have (learn) the ability to encourage others to participate. If you have difficulty in doing this use 'peer pressure' ie when you normally ask for 'volunteers' then always work on the premise that no one will. Have at least a couple of people in mind for the crowdbreakers and 'volunteer' them, asking for a round of applause for the poor unsuspecting individuals. Choose your volunteers carefully so that you do not cause acute embarrassment.

25

3 Be ready to switch to another appropriate game if the one chosen flops!

4 Be prepared for your 'wrap-up' after the game or games if you are using them as a preamble to a talk or discussion.

5 The group must not feel that you are just going through the motions of the activities as a means to an end. They should be enjoyed for their own sake by both you, as the leader, and the group. If you don't enjoy the game then it can almost be guaranteed that this will reflect on the group.

6 Keep to time – do not let your programme drag. Always stop when you are winning.

7 Be casually authoritative. You are not a 'teacher', 'parent', or 'policeman', but an older wiser friend who naturally demands respect! As a general rule, young people want discipline and will feel secure within an informal friendly framework of 'expected behaviour'.

8 Always use a 'programme worksheet' so that you can have a full summary of the total schedule, crowdbreakers, equipment, discussion, reaction, etc.

Study the programme worksheet that I use and how it is filled in. (p. 27).

PROGRAMME WORKSHEET (Example Only)

SUBJECT: The Great Lie : Deceit   DATE: 15 May '83

MAIN OBJECTIVE(S): To show that 'deceit' often easily becomes a habit.
The Bible does not cover up deceit, even in 'godly' people. Truth is opposed to deceit
— practical ways through the problem.

CROWDBREAKER(S):

1 Title Aeroplane Ride
  (Equipment)   Plank ; 3 blindfolds ; a couple of
                bricks to rest the plank on.

2 Title: Marshmallow Stuff
  (Equipment)   3 packets of marshmallows ; 3 chairs
                3 blindfolds and a watch ; Polaroid
                camera ; a glass of water !

3 Title:
  (Equipment)

DISCUSSION/TALK:
  Sources: Bible Passage(s): Jacob and Esau (Gen 27.) ;
                David and Uriah (2 Sam 11)
                Ananias and Sapphira
                            (Acts 5 : 1-11)

  Other(s): Newspaper cuttings that I have
            collected over the last few days.

REACTIONS OF THE GROUP: The 'reaction cards' were
generally very positive. The two crowdbreakers
went well but the 'wrap-up' at the end was
too long — I tried to do too much and read too
many verses.

27

How to use Crowdbreakers

After choosing the games to fit subject:

1 Prepare your game equipment carefully.
2 Practise using the equipment before the event to make sure it works!
3 Know the game inside out. You will not be able to use the book on the day. You can, but the effect is minimal. You must have confidence in your preparation.
4 The presentation and operation of the game must go off with military precision.
5 Know your audience – remember you are not producing the game for your own amusement. Make sure that those you volunteer will accept (eventually) their fate!! *Hint*: teenagers will, generally speaking, go along with a game more than you think they will. Never be afraid to experiment with the variety of games in this book, however messy or seemingly outrageous. Many a time I have been given a group of teenagers to work on and told that they are a very shy and reserved bunch, only to discover that they have been the most enthusiastic, sadistic group that can be imagined.
6 Review each game after using it. Can you improve on it? What was the general response? Are there any practical lessons to be learned for the next time?

Below each Crowdbreaker in the book there is plenty of space to write down your findings.

1
Signature Bingo

Issue everyone with a pencil and piece of paper. The paper must be lined off into squares prior to the event, with just a few less squares than the number you expect to be present. Each person then moves about collecting a different signature in each square. When all the squares on each piece of paper have been filled with signatures, the leader calls out the names of the people present at random, from slips drawn from a bowl. (Earlier the names of every person present have been written on slips of paper and put in a bowl). As each name is called the players check it off on their sheet and the first person to check all the names in any horizontal or vertical row is the winner.

Great for getting things started.

Starter   Chance   Relationships

Equipment: Paper, pencils.

2
Conversation starter

Each person on arriving is given a sheet of paper with various instructions on it for him/her to follow. To do this, everyone must circulate and speak to all those present. This game is a good conversation maker.

Ideas for the list of instruction:

a Count the number of brown-eyed guys in the room.
b Find out who has the strangest hobby.
c Find out who has made the longest trip.
d Try and find out who knows what a trichology is.
e Which girls wear striped pyjamas.
f Who hasn't cleaned their teeth today.

When the lists are complete they are returned to the leader, who then reads out any amusing answers.

Starter   Relationships   Awareness   Embarrassment

Equipment: Paper, pencils.

3
Who Am I?

Prepare beforehand slips of paper on which are written the names of famous people, both present-day and historical. As each person arrives, pin a slip on their back without them knowing what it says. The participants look at each other's slips and then have a conversation with one another as though they were talking with the person named on the slip. As the conversation continues, each one tries to guess who they are supposed to be. The remarks should not be so leading as to give away the identity too soon.

This can be hilariously funny and frustrating. As the leader, how about walking around with a concealed cassette recorder and playing back some of the conversations afterwards?

Starter   Phonies

Equipment: Slips of Paper, Safety Pins

4
Song partners

Write out the names of well-known songs in pairs on slips of paper.
Distribute the slips and, on a given signal, each person begins singing
and whistling his song. The aim is for each person to discover his
partner. If your building has a number of rooms encourage everyone
to march all over the place.

Relationships   Music   Communication

Equipment: Prepared slips of paper

5
Huddles

Everyone sits on the floor. The leader then calls out a number and players must get into groups of that number. Anyone not in a group is considered out. Call a variety of numbers, large and small, depending on the number of players. The formation of groups usually results in a large amount of pushing, pulling, grabbing and laughter. The number of players gradually diminishes, and the game ends when 2 players remain.

Observe their movements so that you can personalise their reaction in discussion later, eg 'Did you see the way Sandra pulled Peter's hair to get into the circle and found out it was his hair-piece . . . ?'

Conformity   Friendships   Change   Violence   Cheating   Conflict

Equipment: None

6
Magical handshakes

Before people gather for the game, secretly give a number of persons (eg 4 to 8) a small bar of chocolate. When everyone is ready to begin, tell them that there are a number of those present who have a bar of chocolate and the tenth person to shake these people by the hand will be given the chocolate. Players must announce their name each time they shake hands. For a token reward, many people who are shy lose their inhibitions and get stuck in.

Variation: Coins of various denominations, fruit, etc. can be used instead of chocolate.

Starter   Chance   Rewards   Relationships   Choice

Equipment: Small bars of chocolate

7
Swap

Form a circle of girls around a circle of guys. Each girl is partnered with a guy. As the music begins the girls move in an anti-clockwise direction, the guys in a clockwise direction. When the music stops each person must grab a partner (must be a different partner from his/her original partner, and must be a different partner each time. Also, at each pause the leader shouts an instruction – eg, 'girls place right shoe in centre of circle and put on guy's right shoe, 'guys give their partner their coat or jumper'). After about six turns, ask everyone to get back with the 'original' partner that they had at the beginning of the game and give a prize for the most 'weird' looking couple. Give a second prize to the couple who can get back to their original state of dress first.

This is best played in winter when there is a lot worn; it becomes a bit more difficult in summer for obvious reasons.

Choice   Fashion

Equipment: Music

8
Dad mum and junior

Prior to the occasion, write surnames on slips of paper, three of each name, and prefix each surname with 'Dad', or 'Mum', or 'Junior', eg 'Dad Smith', 'Mum Smith', 'Junior Smith'. Ensure that the number present will enable each family to be complete. The slips of paper are scattered on the playing area, and on a given signal each player grabs one slip and tries to find his other two family members by shouting out eg 'Dad Jones'. A tremendous amount of noise is guaranteed. On forming their family trio, the group must find a seat, and then sit with 'Dad' at the bottom, then 'Mum' and finally 'Junior' on top. Have a prize for the first trio seated in this fashion. Before breaking this seating arrangement, ensure that players have introduced themselves.

With large numbers this can create an 'atmosphere' for a crazy evening. Once they are in their families you may wish to use this unit as a starter for another game or discussion.

Families   Starter

Equipment: Slips of paper, enough for those attending

9
Song scramble

Prior to the event, the leader writes out several well-known songs, line by line, but writes down only one line on each slip of paper. Use preferably six line songs. The slips are then scattered on the floor. On the given signal each player grabs a slip and tries to find the holders of the other slips which will complete the song. The winning group is the first group to assemble correctly and sing their song. Ensure that only enough songs are used to cover the number of people present. If you have a non-musical group of people all attempting to sing at the same time it can be deafening! It is therefore worth keeping a tape of it, to be used as blackmail or as an illustration on some other suitable occasion.

Friendships   Fellowship   Peer pressure   Conformity

Equipment: Slips of paper

10
Pile up

ALL THOSE WEARING BELTS SHOULD MOVE 3 PLACES TO THEIR RIGHT...

Each person sits on a strong chair in a circle. When the leader calls out a descriptive phrase, all players to whom this applies must move in the direction nominated by the leader, eg, 'All girls with blonde hair move to the chair 3 places to the right'. If someone already occupies the chair, the person simply sits on top of the player (or players) already there. Whenever a player sitting under another player (or players) is obliged to move, then all players on top of him move also. Thus it can be visualized that as the game proceeds, many players get stacked onto one chair, much to the joy and agony of those involved.

Can you beat eleven on one chair? If so the girl who was on the bottom of the stack would like to correspond and share similar experiences!

Suffering   Loneliness   Conformity

Equipment: Chairs

11
Rhyming names

Everyone sits in a circle, and one person begins by announcing his name with a brief rhyming description of himself, eg 'I'm Jack, I'm as sharp as a tack', 'I'm Bob, a great fat slob'. The next person quotes the first person's rhyme, and then adds his own. The next person states the previous two rhymes and adds his own. So it goes on around the circle. This game can be quite hilarious and certainly helps people to remember names.

If you can encourage humorous rhymes by starting with yourself, this will produce interesting results. Get someone to write them down for future reference!

Awareness   Humour   Personality

Equipment: None

12
Descriptive partners

Each guy is introduced to a girl, and asked to write a short description of this girl as he sees her, but without stating her name. He must not refer to the colours of her clothes as this will be too obvious. When everyone has completed this task, all the slips are collected and mixed up in a bowl. Then each guy selects a slip and must find the girl he thinks fits the description.

Variation:
        1 Have the first guy draw a picture of the girl.
        2 Do the same but have the girl describing the
          boy.

Caution: For obvious reasons you must know your group very well for this one to go 'right', and not give offence.

Relationships   *Sex/Dating*   *Awareness*   *Perception*   *Embarrassment*

Equipment: paper and pencils

13
Ball and chain

Each player is given a blown-up balloon with a piece of string attached, which he ties around his ankle to give a ball and chain effect. On a given signal, each player attempts to stamp on other people's balloons attempting to burst them while protecting his own balloon. Players retire on losing their balloon, and the winner is the last person remaining.

Variations:

> 1 Divide the people up into pairs, with the balloon attached to the girl's ankle; the guy's role being to protect his partner.
>
> 2 Each player has the balloon tied around his waist so the balloon lags behind. He also has a paper waddle. The object is the same, ie destruction of everyone else's balloon, while protecting your own. However, the leader must make sure that the paper waddles are the only weapons used.

This game surprisingly takes very little time. I suggest that either the girls take off their high-heeled shoes or you don't play.

Fear   Aggression   Violence   Conflict   Pain

Equipment: Balloons, and pieces of string, 1 metre in length

14
Aerial balloon contest

Every person is given a balloon. After it is blown up, it is thrown into the air, and while trying to keep it afloat as long as possible, each player at the same time attempts to knock other people's balloons to the floor. The object is to see whose balloon will stay in the air the longest.

N.B. Balloons will need to have some form of identification, eg, the initials of each of the contestants written on the inflated balloon in felt tip pen.

Variation:

Divide into couples with one balloon between them.

A lot of cheating goes on in this game even in the best balloon circles.

Weakness Aggression Cheating Survival

Equipment: Balloons

15
Burst it

The group is divided into two teams. One team is called the 'destroyers', and the other the 'defenders'. A balloon is tossed up, and the destroyers attempt to break it by any means, while the defenders try to protect it. The time taken before it is destroyed is recorded. When the balloon is burst, the defenders become the destroyers. Each group is given four turns in each role (or throw four balloons into the air simultaneously) and the winner is the group with the smallest total time.
Variation:
      Try this using heads only to destroy and defend.
Those of weak constitution die very quickly in a game of this nature. Each turn will only last a few seconds.

Violence   Aggression   War

Equipment: Balloons

16
Balloon netball

Players are divided into equal teams. a goalie for each team armed with a pin, is standing on a chair stationed at either end of the room. The object of each team is to push and knock the balloon towards their goalie. A goal is scored each time the goalie bursts the balloon.
Variation:

> If you want to economise, substitute a bucket,
> etc., to catch the balloons in instead of using a
> pin.

I suggest you pick tall goalies or high chairs, otherwise pins in the wrong places can be quite dangerous.

Competitive spirit   Teamwork   Leadership

Equipment: 2 chairs, 2 pins and a supply of balloons

17
Balloon corner ball

Players are divided into two teams, distinguished by blue and red arm bands or coloured tape on their foreheads. Four goals are created by stretching wool across the four corners of the room, a little more than 2 metres above the floor. The goals in the diagonally opposite corners are in the same colour (blue or red). With players scattered throughout the playing area, two balloons are thrown up, one blue, the other red. The game consists of each team trying to hit their coloured balloon through their coloured goals, while keeping their opponents from scoring with their balloon. Any time a goal is scored both balloons are thrown up in the centre. Have a supply of blown-up balloons ready to replace any burst balloons. The winner is the team scoring the highest number of goals in a pre-determined time period.

If you can choose teams that are totally unbalanced, so that the same team is always scoring, you can create very strong feelings of frustration and strength, ready for a useful discussion on the subjects given.

Awareness   Conflict   Strength   Frustration   Tension

Equipment: A supply of wool and balloons in both red and blue

18
Balloon volleyball

Divide the group into two teams. Stretch a net across a room about 2.5 metres above the floor. Using the balloons as a ball, each team tries to keep the balloon from touching the floor on their side. Each team is allowed only to hit the balloon a maximum of five times on their side.

This game can be spoilt if you play it for too long and allow it to drag.

Trust   Loyalty   Teamwork

Equipment: Balloons and net

19
Pirates

Divide the players into four equal teams, with each team sitting in a corner of the room, with a small circle drawn in front of each team. The seven objects are placed in a circle in the centre of the room. Team members are numbered from one upwards. The leader calls out a number eg, '6', and the four players whose number is '6' run to the centre circle and pick up an object and bring it back to their team's circle. Only one object can be picked up at a time, and it must be placed in the circle not thrown. They then return to the circle and pick up another object and place that in their circle. They keep returning to the centre circle until all the objects are gone, and then they begin pirating objects (one at a time) from opponents' circles. This continues until one player has four objects in his circle. This 'pirate' then scores one point for his team. The leader calls other numbers, and the team with the most points at the end wins.

This is a fast moving, and energetic game that creates team spirit as well as negative feelings of cheating and revenge – excellent!

Cheating   Revenge   Loyalty   Sin   Greed

Equipment: 7 small objects (stones or cans or shoes), chalk

20
Harem

A variation of the 'Pirates' game. Each team is replaced by a solitary guy, and eight girls are placed in the centre instead of objects. The guys must pick up the girl and place her in his corner. The aim is the same as pirates, with the winner being the one who ends up with three girls.

This is OK if your girls are not tooooooooo big and your guys are not too weeeeeeee.

Cheating   Aggression   Weakness

Equipment: None

21
King of the circle

Make a circle with a radius of seven feet. Place a dozen guys inside it. At a given signal each tries to push everybody else out, while trying to stay in himself. Once a guy is pushed out of the circle, he retires from the game. The last person to stay in the circle wins.

Variation:

FEMALE SUPREMACY – Place all the guys in a circle and have the girls surround the circle. On the given signal, the girls see how long it takes to push, pull, drag, etc. all the guys from inside the circle. The guys cannot fight back in any way. They can only cling to each other for defence.

If you have guys that say that they are not afraid of the girls then try the variation and stand well back and . . . it's too ghastly for the printed page.

Violence   Aggression   Frustration   Strength   Weakness

Equipment: none

22
Musical chairs

This is an old favourite which continues to maintain its popularity. Chairs are arranged in two lines, back to back, with players sitting on them. As the music starts, players get up and move round the chairs in a clockwise direction. The leader removes at least one chair. When the music stops each player must find a chair. Those without a chair drop out of the game.

Variation

1 *Couple musical chairs* – same as above, except the game starts with one chair per couple. The girl sits on the guy's lap. As the music starts, the girls move clockwise and the guys move anti-clockwise. When the music stops the guy must seat himself with a girl on his knee. Original pairs do not need to reform.

2 *Blindfold Musical Chairs* – Blindfold the guy who sits on the girl's lap. As the music starts, she guides her partner around the chairs. When the music stops the girls finds a seat and guides the guy to it and seats him on her knee.

3 *Musical Football* – The players are seated in a closed circle, facing out. There are just enough chairs for the seated players. The leader then goes around the circle and gives each player the name of some object, person or movement connected with football. The leader or someone else stands in the centre of the circle, and acts out the role of sports commentator by broadcasting a football game in typical radio style, becoming more and more excited over the progress of the game. Whenever a player hears his object or movement mentioned he jumps up and begins moving around the circle clockwise. Chairs are removed from the circle. As soon as the com-

mentator mentions the word 'Fumble', everyone
must dash for a seat, and the players failing to
secure seats are out. Much of the success of the
game depends on the skill of the commentator.
The leader should prepare a list of football teams
on a card so that there will be no delay in naming
the players and in the commentary.
Keep these moving fast to avoid boredom – always be thinking up
variations to these variations so that you can end up with a variation of
a variation of a variation of a variation . . .

Frustration   Awareness   Failure

*Equipment: A pile of single chairs, music, list of football teams,
players and commentary*

23
Spring tussle

This is a good puzzle teaser. Divide the group into couples, and give each pair two pieces of string. The girl ties one end to her right wrist and the other to her left. Partner repeats the process but, before tying, crosses his string over his partner's string. The object is to find the first pair to untangle the strings without breaking the string or wriggling the string off the hand.

Solution:
> Make a loop in your string, and slide it under the
> string tied around you partner's wrist and over
> his hand.

To see this in action is to believe it – weird and wonderful positions. A camera is a must if you can hold it still enough with laughing so much.

Frustration   Dating   Cheating

Equipment: 1 metre long pieces of string

24
Fruit salad

Players form a square and sit down. The leader goes round the square allocating people as 'apple', 'banana', or 'orange'. When the leader yells one of the fruits, eg 'bananas', all those allocated bananas must cross the floor and find a seat vacated by another 'banana'. The last person to find a seat is out, and the chair is removed. Any combination of fruits can be called, and if 'fruit salad' is called, everyone must change places.

Differences   Attitudes

Equipment: None

25
Scalps

Give each player a paper bag to fit on his head with slits so that they can see out. On the signal, each person tries to see how many scalps he can collect without losing his own. When a person loses his scalp he is out of the game. Scalps may not be held on the head by the hand, they may be protected only by fast footwork or dodging. The last to remain, or to collect the largest number of scalps (in a certain time) is the winner.

Variation:

> Try the same game with the participants hopping
> or with their legs tied together

Suggestion: Ask your group to write on their bags something about their personalities that is not too personal eg, shy, strong, etc. If you then play the game you can have a very useful discussion on the real you. Who am I? etc.

Life   Personality

Equipment: A paper bag and felt tip pen per person

26
Snake dodge

Everyone stands in a circle except seven players who form a snake in the centre. Everyone except the front person of the snake, holds the wrist of the person in front. The ball is given to the players who make up the circle. The ball is tossed about by the players in the circle and when possible it is thrown at the 'tail' of the snake. The snake in the circle moves about attempting to protect the tail. When the tail person is struck below the knee, he joins the circle and the second last person in the snake becomes the new tail. Gradually the snake is shortened until only one player remains. Several teams of seven can be formed and a competition conducted to find which team can last the longest.

In combination with other discussion stimulus this game can be very helpful in introducing the subject of 'friends'; why we need them, what happens when they leave us and let us down etc.

Friendships   Protection   Loneliness

Equipment: Basketball

27
Snake tails

Form 'snake' teams of 6–10 players. The snakes formed by players holding the waist of the person in front (except the first person). The tail person of the 'snake' tucks a handkerchief under his belt at the back to form a tail. On the signal to start each snake attempts to grab the tails from the other snakes without losing his own. Only the head of each snake can make the grabs. The more snakes, the more hilarious the 'pile up' result.

An amazing game.

Fellowship   Working together

Equipment: Handkerchief per team

28
Dog and the bone

An old game which still maintains its popularity. The players are divided into two equal teams, sitting on chairs (in lines 3 metres apart), facing each other. They number off down the lines, each team beginning at the opposite end. Midway between the two teams the 'bone' (ball or quoit) is placed on the floor.

The leader calls out a number. Players with this number in both teams dash forward, and try to snatch the 'bone' and get back to their seat without being tagged by their opponent. The player who succeeds gains a point for his team, but if he is tagged the opposition gains the point. Games often develop into a cunning exercise, where players move their hands very close to the 'bone' without actually touching it, until one can catch the other momentarily off-guard.

Deceit

Equipment: A quoit or ball

29
Sudden death

Excellent game for a group of energetic teenagers. Players join hands in a circle around a mat. Then by pulling, pushing and tugging, each player tries to make someone else step onto the mat, without doing so himself. Players drop out of the game once they touch the mat. If the circle breaks, the two players who 'let go' must drop out.

If you have a group that needs to lose energy then a couple of games of this does the job. If you feel that you need to show who's in charge and you are convinced that you are going to win, play it yourself.

Aggression   Strength

Equipment: Mat

30
Snowball Fight

Form two teams. Separate the teams by a row of chairs, and give each team a huge stack of newspaper. On the signal to start, the object of each team is to roll the paper into balls and throw as many paper balls as possible on the other team's side within a time limit. The team with the most paper on their side loses. Each team can defend his side from the opposing snowballs.

Watch for cheating – snowballs being dropped into no-man's land or thrown back after being successfully thrown onto their side.

War

Equipment: Unlimited supply of newspaper

31
The vacant wink

Chairs are arranged in a circle facing inwards. Girls sit on the chairs except one which is left vacant. Behind all the chairs including the empty one, stands a guy with his hands resting on the top of the chair but not touching the girl sitting on it. The guy behind the empty chair starts the game by winking at one of the girls who must immediately try to leave her chair and dash to the empty one. However the guy behind her chair must try and stop her from leaving by putting his hands on her shoulders. If she succeeds in getting away, the guy who failed to keep her must then wink at some other girl in order to fill the chair in front of him. The winking guy must use guile and aim to obtain surprise. After a while, change over and have the girls do the winking.

This game is great fun if you encourage speed winking. Don't hesitate to use the couple arrangement, either for another game or discussion. Please remember that any discussion on the subject needs very careful and sensitive handling.

Dating   Relationships   Emotions   Attraction

Equipment: None

32
Death wink

The group sit in a large circle facing inward. A playing card is given to each player, one of the cards being a joker. No one knows who has the joker but the game commences with the holder of the joker attempting to kill as many of the players as possible by discreetly winking at them. Once a person has been winked at he must die by falling off the chair or collapsing in a heap on the floor with loud blood-curdling screams! However if he is seen by one of the players when winking at somebody else the player stops the game by raising a hand and declaring that the murderer is . . . . If he is wrong he must immediately commit suicide. If he is right the game is concluded, the number dead counted and the cards reshuffled. The winner is the murderer who has killed the most at the end of the game.

Needs to be done quickly to keep interest.

Death   Sly

Equipment: Pack of cards

33
Bosses and secretaries

Arrange players into couples, with each of the partners at opposite sides of the room. Use all the walls so that the players are spaced around the hall. One member of each couple (the boss) is given a prepared newspaper cutting (use six different messages of approximately the same length), while the other member (secretary) has a piece of paper and a pencil. On the signal to start the bosses begin dictating the contents of the newspaper cutting to the secretaries who try to take it down. This is a difficult task with so many competing voices. The first couple with a complete correct message of dictation are the winners.

Variation:

       To make it more difficult have the bosses sucking
       a lolly, standing on a chair on one leg.

If you can get quite a crowd doing this, it can be used to express a great deal on the subject of communication, rumours, what is true, etc.

Work   Communication   Truth   Bible

Equipment: Paper, pencils and prepared statements

34
Crows and cranes

Draw a line down the centre of the room. Divide players into two teams. Teams then stand in a line on opposite sides of the drawn line. All players face the front looking at the leader and place one foot on the line touching the foot of an opposing player. Designate one team 'crows', the other 'cranes'. The leader then calls one of the two words, 'crow' or 'cranes'. He does this by stressing the 'cr-cr-cr' so that both sides will be in suspense, not knowing if crows or cranes will be called. When one of the names is called, that team turns and runs to its side wall. The other team chases and tries to touch as many opponents as possible. Those caught are 'out'. The leader also may call anything else besides the command words, eg 'crabs, crocodiles, crayfish, etc. Players who move when this happens are also 'out'. When one team eliminates all the other team, the game is over.
Variation:
  Substitute team names 'rats' and 'rabbits'. Words
  other than command words may be 'rattlesnakes',
  'rockets'.

Communication

Equipment: None

63

35
Indoor Hockey

Another 'oldie' that maintains its popularity. Teams form up on opposite sides of the hall. The players in each team are numbered, starting from opposite ends. The leader calls out a number and the appropriate person in each team races to the centre, picks up the nearest stick and pushes or hits the quoit (or ball) towards his team's goal. When a goal is scored the sticks and quoit are returned to the centre. Goals may be formed by two chairs, legs of bench, chalk marks on the floor.

Vary this by asking them to hop, jump, run backwards, crawl, etc. to give it that 'extra'.

Goal setting   Strategy

Equipment: goals, 2 sticks and a small rubber ball or quoit.

36
Donkey rounders

Divide the players into two teams who line up at opposite sides of the table. The server strikes the ball over the net, drops the bat on to the table and then runs round the table to join the end of his team at the opposite side, while the next player picks up the bat and gets the return by the players from the other team. Each player relinquishes the bat as soon as he has made his play. As a player fouls a shot he is given a letter of the word 'donkey', and after 6 fouls his 'donkey' is complete and he drops out. Fouls are achieved as in normal table tennis rules.

Keep this moving for maximum hilarity, excitement and tension.

Failure

Equipment: Table tennis table, net, 2 bats and a table tennis ball

37
Knights, cavaliers and horsemen

Form the group into partners and explain three movements.

1 When the leader yells 'knights' the guy goes down on one knee and the girl sits on his knee.

2 When the leader yells 'horsemen', the guy goes down on all fours like a horse, and the girl sits on him.

3 When the leader yells 'cavaliers', the guy must pick up the girl into his arms.

The pairs move around the floor until the leader calls out any of these movements. The last pair to form the stance are out. The leader may call out these movements in any combination and very quickly before stopping. Whenever the leader yells 'change' the roles are reversed in the next movement, eg, if the leader yells 'cavaliers' next the girl picks up the guy.

It is a simple elimination game with the winner being the last pair to remain, that is if they haven't already collapsed with exhaustion.

Courtesies   Role changing – boy/girl   Historical Tradition

Equipment: None

38
Group Collection

Put the players into groups of five or six. The groups sit in their own circles around the room. Each group selects a runner. The leader places himself in the centre of the room and begins to call for objects. The group must find the object (preferably from within the group) and gives it to their runner who gets it to the leader. The first group who does this with each object called scores one point. Have a list of about 20 objects of amusing variety eg, 9 cm blonde hair, the smallest pair of socks in the group, exactly £1.57.

Variation:

    1 The messenger has his feet tied together.

    2 The messenger carries the recipient of the
       object

    3 the messenger hops or jumps

Group excitement and tension builds up with this game if it moves fast and the objects asked for are different to the norm or asked for in an indirect way. As you can imagine this has many discussion possibilities.

Giving   Excitement   Materialism   Group Feelings   Enthusiasm

Equipment: None

39
Shoot it out!

Two 'candle hats' are constructed out of paper plates, ribbon and the two short candles (the candle is secured with wax on top of the upside down plate). Ribbon is used to tie the hat on the head of the person. The two players wearing the 'candle hats' are given water pistols and placed 3–3½ metres apart. Their task is to have a duel and see who can be the first to squirt out the other's lighted candle.

This is a must – it's crazy, it's imaginative and everyone wants to have a go. STOP just when everyone is going nuts about having a turn – if you dare!

Fun   Laughter   Enjoyment

Equipment: 2 paper plates, 2 short candles, 2 water pistols, ribbon, matches

40
Wheelbarrow munch

Couples form into wheelbarrows, with the girls doing the wheeling. The object of the game is for the girls to wheel their male partner from one end of the room to the finishing line at the other end. However, their barrow (i.e. the guys) must eat a number of things along the course, e.g. jelly babies, peanuts, marshmallows, small cakes, crisps etc. Make sure the food is placed on clean pieces of paper.

Try doing it again, but blindfold the wheelbarrow. You need a camera for the occasion.

Food – use of   Guidance   Control

Equipment: A range of small eatable delights, blindfolds.

41
Wine making!

Place the grapes in the two bowls. Have two guys compete to see who can make the most juice with his bare feet. Pour the juice into jars to measure the winner. Set a time limit and 'threaten' that the loser must drink the winner's wine.

For maximum effect follow through with your threat. If you want to build the image of your group then stunts like this are musts and you must publicise your event accordingly, eg 'Loser drinks all'.

Winning   Losing   Drinking

Equipment: 2 large plastic bowls, grapes

42
Wetwon

Have five guys lie down on their backs holding a bottle on their foreheads. On the signal a female partner tries to fill the bottle from a bucket using a sponge. The first couple to fill the bottle is the winner.
Variation:
>   Have the girls blindfolded and let them pour the
>   water from a cup, the guy giving the instructions.
Either way the guys are going to end up wet! (Make sure towels are covering their shirts). This really is an outside game if water if going to flow freely, which of course is the main aim – as long as you are not the one on the ground. Very good for those who are going steady – a test of true love.

Sadism   Friendships   Guidance   Frustration

Equipment: Large clear bottles, sponges, buckets of water, cup, towels, blindfolds

43
Blind feeding

This is an old favourite which never ceases to amuse. Arrange couples around a small table and blindfold each player. A plate of feeding mixture is placed on the table and every player is equipped with a spoon. On the signal to start each couple begin feeding each other from their own spoon, the winners being the first couple to empty the plate. Make sure their clothes are adequately protected, and warn against wild movements of the spoons as this can result in broken teeth. If possible use plastic spoons. An offer of a shampoo sachet is often very welcome!
Variation:
      Have each couple cleaning each other's teeth

The devil   Guidance   Help   Faith   Trust

Equipment: Blindfolds, plates of feeding mixture (eg. ice cream, custard) spoons.

44
Balloon shaving

Select four couples. Have the male member of each couple seated on a chair with the neck of an inflated and tied balloon in his mouth, and a towel draped around his front. The balloon is then covered with shaving cream and at a given signal the female member attempts to shave it off with a razor blade. It causes much suspense and amusement, especially if the balloon bursts. I always find that a pin slipped into the girl's hand during the proceedings is very often helpful to explode the tension created. Also, the beauty of this game is that the girl thinks that the explosion is going to create a mess over 'him' but . . . Well, play the game and find out what really happens!
Variation:
      If you have very feminine girls then reverse the roles!

Tension   Scheming   Trust   Deceit (pins)

Equipment: 4 razor blades, 4 balloons, shaving cream, towels and 4 pins

45
Jousting

Two players are given two tablespoons and an orange each. In the one hand each player must hold one tablespoon with his orange balanced on it. In the other hand he holds the second tablespoon, which he uses both to defend himself and to knock his opponent's orange from his tablespoon.

Variation:
> Have teams rather than individuals contesting or a number of contestants at the same time but 'each man for himself'.

Fighting   Winning   Getting the Balance

Equipment: 4 tablespoons, 2 oranges

46
Balancing pillow fight

Place the boxes about one metre apart. Place a player on each box and give them each a pillow. At the signal to start the players begin to rain blows on their opponent, the winner being the first player to force the other to lose balance and fall off. Play quarter and semi-finals to get your champion. Build this up with a commentary about the pillows, contestants' boxes (now made small and higher), etc.

Maximum publicity with outside teams, etc, would give an impetus to your activities on that occasion.

A commentary on life

Equipment: 2 boxes of equal size, 2 pillows

47
Banana duel

Two players stand back to back, each with a banana in his pocket. On the signal to begin both draw out their banana and try to peel it one-handed, trying to be the first to turn around and squash it in the other player's face. A very messy game, but very popular.

Materialism   Difficulty

Equipment: 2 bananas

48
Chocolate feast

Everyone sits in a large circle, with a table in the centre, on which is the plate with chocolates on it, knife and fork arranged, and the scarf, hat and gloves lying on a chair near the table. Two dice are passed around the circle, with everyone taking turns in thowing. When a player throws a double four, five or six he dashes to the table, puts on the hat, gloves scarf and begins to eat the chocolate with a knife and fork. As soon as another player throws any of the above combinations he takes the items off the first player, puts them on himself and starts eating the chocolates until someone throws another combination. The game continues until all the chocolates have been eaten.
Variation:
> Use other well-liked confectionary instead of chocolates, or to slow the eating down use toffees.

Greed   Chance

Equipment: 2 boxes of chocolates, knife, fork, plate, gloves,
scarf, hat, 2 dice, table and chair

49
Flour mould

Place a mould of flour on a table covered by a newspaper. (The mould is formed by pressing flour into a container, inverting it and lightly tapping the base). On top of the mould place a cherry. Place the knife beside the mould. Begin to call out different descriptions and anyone fitting that description must come out and cut a slice of the mould without the cherry falling from the top. Examples of descriptions: 'all redheaded girls', 'anyone wearing belts'. The person who causes the cherry to fall must retrieve the cherry from the collapsed pile of flour using only their mouth and with their hands behind their backs.

Three suggestions: (1) always have a 'spare' flour mould in case of mishaps or vandalism. (2) Try cutting the mould holding the knife handle with your teeth as a variation to the above. (3) Never offer a towel to clean the face of the individual. Take the attitude that you expect them to spend the evening with flour on their face. This may be essential to your discussion subject.

Attitudes   Prejudice   Fear

Equipment: 1 kg. of flour, knife, newspaper, container, a cherry

50
Mummification

Select three couples. Provide each girl with two toilet rolls and tell her to make an Eyptian Mummy out of her partner. The winning couple is the first to complete the task, provided no skin or clothing is left showing.

Evidence of the Bible   Cover up . . . of truth   Culture   Death

Equipment: 6 toilet rolls.

51
Eggskill

Select four couples. The guy lies down on his back and holds a paper cup in his mouth with a towel draped over his shoulders. Each girl must stand without bending over the guy, break an egg and drop the contents into the cup. Egg shampoo is very popular and does wonders for the hair.

Fear   Direction   Consequences

Equipment: 4 eggs, paper cups, towels

52
Egg blow

Crack a raw egg into clear plastic tubing and put a guy at each end. Guys must blow egg at each other until one or other 'gets it'. Loser will usually be the guy who has to take a breath first.

Variation:

> Use water instead, although this is not so volatile
> and messy!

Power

Equipment: 1.5 metres length of 2.5 cm. plastic (clear) tubing, 1 egg

53
Balloon hugging

Select couples who are each given three balloons. On the signal to start the couple must blow up the three balloons and place two of the balloons under the girl's armpits and have her sit on the third. The guy tries to help in breaking the three balloons simultaneously by hugging the girl. The winning couple is the first couple to burst the three balloons.

Believing is seeing this in action.

Dating

Equipment: 3 balloons per participating couples

55
Egg obstacle race

Select an 'hysterical' type girl. Scatter two dozen eggs on the floor and indicate to her that her job is to walk from one end of the room to the other through the field of eggs, blindfolded. While blindfolding her, have some members quietly pick up the eggs and cover the floor in cornflakes. Background noise may be needed to hide the sound of the operation. When the girl is blindfolded give her an egg to carry in her hand, and warn her not to become tense and squeeze it as she will get egg's contents all over her hand. (This is a special egg which has had a whole poked in it, its contents drained out and the egg filled with water). Allow the girl to begin to move from one end to the other. If adequate cornflakes have been used, each step will bring a crunching sound (very similar to stepping on eggs, especially if she believes eggs are there!) The girl is usually a wreck by the time she has reached the end, especially if the audience has been primed to groan with her every step. As she reaches the end, the leader congratulates her by shaking and squeezing her hand containing the egg she was carrying. This is usually the last straw!

Fear   Hysteria   Deceit

Equipment: 2 dozen eggs, large packet of cornflakes, blindfold

56
Kiss the magic book

A victim is 'dragged' before the group on a false and exaggerated charge and told that he can only gain the forgiveness of the group by kissing the magic book three times. He is shown the book on a table, then blindfolded and allowed to kiss the book a first and second time. As he prepares to kiss the book a third time a saucer of flour is placed on the book and the victim gets a mouthful!

Deceit Fairness Judgement Punishment

Equipment: Blindfold, book and saucer of flour

57
Aeroplane Ride

A very old snare that still causes amusement. Select a girl who has never been for a trip in an aircraft. Blindfold her and have her stand on a plank which is resting on several bricks. Tell her that she is going up in the air and to duck as she gets higher so she does not hit the ceiling. Indicate that she can have the support of two guys whose shoulders she can use to lean on. Two strong guys then take hold of the ends of the plank and slowly raise it.

They only actually raise it a couple of centimetres, but at the same time the 'support' guys begin to stoop so that the rider begins to crouch thinking she is quite high. The leader then tells the rider to jump. However the rider should have a feeling of great height and will hesitate, and will need much encouragment from the audience. When she does jump the sudden landing will surprise her. *Warning*: There must be somebody in front to catch the falling body!
Variation:

    1 The two guys can go up and down to give effect.

    2 Place a heavy book above the rider's head and arrange for the head to hit it at some stage of the proceedings giving the impression that they have hit the ceiling!

Deceit   Trust   Belief

Equipment: A plank, bricks, blindfold

58
Thief

Have ten guys line up in a straight line, all facing in the same direction, with their shoulders touching. The leader stands at the end of the line. The leader begins by saying: 'I saw a dog'. The next person asks 'Where?' and the leader replies 'Over there' and points with his right arm. The second person then says 'I saw a dog' and the third person asks 'Where?' and the second person says 'Over there' and points in the direction of the leader's arm. It is essential that the arms are left outstretched. This question-answer dialogue goes right down the line. Then the leader begins again and starts off by pointing with the left arm. After the line finishes the dialogue, the leader starts a new dialogue and has the group squatting down in answer to 'Where?'. The end result is that the line of guys are squatting down and pointing in the same direction with both arms. Finally the leader says 'I saw a dog' and on the second person asking 'Where?', he suddenly shoves the second player sharply and says 'There'. As a result the whole line of guys goes down like a pack of cards. It is important that the guys maintain a straight line through the stunt. Only do this if you can maintain a friendship afterwards with your group.

Trust   Deceit   Attitudes   Influence

Equipment: None

59
The Queen of Sheba

Select a guy who does not know this snare, and send him from the room. Then select eight guys who form two lines (four on either side) down the hall to a chair on which is seated the belle of the group – the 'Queen of Sheba'. The innocent male is brought into the room, and the leader conveys in very flowery language what a lucky guy he is, because he has been given the rare honour of being introduced to the Queen of Sheba, who will accord him the privilege of a kiss. However he must earn the kiss and thus he must be blindfolded and pass down the corridor of 'guards' who are armed with paper tubes. Blindfolded the victim begins the ordeal and on making it through the line of guards is kissed by a hairy bearded guy who is substituted for the Queen, or the Queen herself now wearing a false beard – that is unless you have some bearded girls in your group. Make sure the guards are light with their blows.

Relationships – Homosexual – Dating   Deceit

Equipment: 8 paper tubes, blindfold

60
Drying the floor

The victim is induced to sit on the floor with his legs spread wide apart, with a pool of water between his feet. He is armed with a paper tube. The leader approaches with a large towel in his hand and claims that he will be able to wipe up the water before the victim can hit him. Suddenly he grasps the ankles of the victim and slides him forward through the pool of water wiping up the water! Make sure that you pick somebody who can take this!

Perception – the way people look at situations   Deceit

Equipment: Water, towel, paper tube

61
Loaded mousetraps

Divide the group into teams. First person in each team must carry a loaded well oiled mousetrap to a certain line and back and then pass it on to the next person who carries it to the line and back again. This process is repeated down the team. If the trap springs (this will occur often), that player must start again. The team who finishes first are all given a knob of cheese as a reward.

Fear   Surprise   Pain

Equipment: Mousetrap per team, cheese

62
Paper rolling

Divide group into teams. The first person in each team is given a roll of toilet paper. At the signal to start he begins unrolling the roll by passing it over his head to the next person (the first member holds the end). when the roll reaches the end, it is passed back down the row of players under their legs, and on reaching the front, the process is repeated until the roll runs out. If the toilet paper breaks the team is disqualified.

If you know the whereabouts of an old toilet seat, have it gold painted and presented as an award.

Working Together   Dependency

Equipment: Toilet roll per team

63
Stripper relay

This is an ideal relay for a swimming pool. Check first with the attendant that he has no objections to the game. Line up the teams at one end of the pool and a suit of old clothes at the other end. After the signal to start, the first person swims to the other end, climbs out, puts the clothes on and swims back. He then strips off the clothes and gives the clothes to the next person who puts them on and swims to the other end, strips and returns. The process is repeated by the rest of the team. *Precaution must be taken that every player is an adequate swimmer* and that a qualified lifesaver is on hand. Played in a room/hall with players running, the game can still evoke a great amount of fun.

Fashion   Restriction

Equipment: A collection of baggy clothes per team (at least a skirt and a pair of trousers)

64
Strawpea

Each player in each team is given a straw. The first person in each team is given a pea, and by drawing in his breath, he can hold the pea on the end of his straw. The next player puts his straw against the pea and draws in his breath. The next carries on and the first withdraws his breath. This technique is repeated down the team; the person at the end of the line walks up to the front and repeats the whole process again until everybody has walked to the front. If a pea drops at any time, the pea must be brought back to the beginning of the line.

This is a great discussion starter on patience and frustration.

Patience   Frustration   Witnessing

Equipment: Straws, dry peas

65
Wheelbarrow and ball race

Each team is divided into pairs who in turn race in wheelbarrow fashion toward the goal line and back to their team, with the addition that the person on his hands pushes a ball along with his head. Although this can be exciting it is also very strenuous, and therefore could possibly be a useful link to the Christian life – i.e., progress very often includes hard work and discipline and that God does not always take us from A-B in a straight line.

Growth   Guidance   Discipline

Equipment; A ball per team

66
The great chicken race

A relay in which couples participate. The girl jumps on to the back of the blindfolded guy and guides him through an obstacle course by giving him any directions she can. To make it a little more difficult, she is handicapped by holding a raw egg in her mouth! An excellent 'starter' for talking about the obstacles that are placed before us in the Christian life that tempt and challenge us towards hopefully, Christian maturity.

Temptation   Challenge . . . in the Christian life   Obstacles to growth

Equipment: Articles for an obstacle course (chairs, ladders, tables, ropes, etc) eggs and blindfolds

67
Dizzy circle

This amusing relay race is best run in two separate circles of the same size in order to avoid collision between players of rival teams who are in no condition to help themselves. Each team makes a circle with the players standing one long space apart, each player in the team facing in the same direction around the circle.

When the signal is given to start the leaders of the two teams run completely around each of the other players in their circle in turn, starting with the player nearest him. It takes a steady head to accomplish this quickly and correctly, as the player doing the circling must not touch any player being circled. If they touch any player during the proceedings they must return to their place and start again. Most players are forced to slow down or stop for a moment at some part of the circle on the way round. When the first player gets back to his original position, he touches the second runner, who starts out over the same course. Any team that finishes on its feet is a good team whether it is the winner or not. There is a strong possibility that some players may not complete the course and die on the sidelines!

Balance as a Christian   Knowing God's will – running around in circles

Equipment: None

68
Musical relay

Have teams seated in rows. Number the players off in each team and allocate to each member the name of a well-known song. A pianist or accordionist is required who plays the tune of one of the songs. On recognising the tune the person allocated that song stands up and dashes to the other end of the room around a chair, and back to their team and sits down. However, when a certain general tune (eg, the National Anthem) is played, the whole team must dash around the chair and back to their seats. Teams score one point for each win and these are accumulated for a final score.

In tune with God   Recognition of God

Equipment: Music, chairs

69
Over and under

Place twenty objects at the feet of the first person in each team. On the signal to start the first person begins passing the objects, one at a time, over his head to the next person. The objects are gradually passed down the team. Having reached the last person, they are passed under the legs of the players, back to the first person who places them on the ground in front of him. It is an amusing relay due to the co-ordination difficulties.

Variation:

    1 Using something like Lego, ask the first person to take down a given construction piece by piece and rebuild as the pieces are returned.

    2 Make the objects very large and very small, eg a blown up beach ball and a pin.

Bible Understanding   Witnessing

Equipment: 20 objects per team (cans or balls or stones)

70
Balloons to buckets

Divide the group into teams. Place a bucket in front of each team at the far end of the room. Give the first person in each team a balloon and a paper tube. On the signal, the first person in each team begins hitting the balloon with the paper tube towards their bucket at the other end of the room. On reaching the bucket, he must get the balloon into the bucket with the tube. On getting the balloon into the bucket he dashes back to his team and gives the balloon and the tube to the next person who in turn does the same, and so on until everybody in the team has had a turn. Players *can* interfere with other teams' balloons which adds to the difficulty. The team finished first is the winner. Have a plentiful supply of balloons blown up.

Patience   Devil (interfering)

Equipment: Paper tubes, balloons, buckets

71
Orange chin pass

This is an old relay that still causes much amusement. Teams are arranged with alternating guys and girls. On the signal, the first person hugs under his chin an orange and then turns to the girl behind him and, without using his hands, must transfer the orange to beneath her chin, and so on, to the last person in the team. Should the orange at any stage drop, it goes back to the person under whose chin it was last held. If it is a hot day, and your activities are outside, why not try a wet sponge instead of an orange?

Teamwork   Friendships

Equipment: An orange per team

72
Bucket brigade

Teams line up with a bucket of water at the head of the team and an empty bucket at the end of the team. On the signal, the first person fills up his cup with water from the bucket, he then pours this water into the cup of the second player. This player pours the water from his cup into that of the next player, and so on down the line until the last player empties his cup into the empty bucket. Meanwhile, the first member continues sending down cups of water as rapidly as possible. The object is to be the first team to transfer the water from the full bucket, cup by cup, down the line to the other bucket. Any team spilling water must be penalised.

Another good game for a hot summer's day that is guaranteed to get a few people wet.

Holy Spirit

Equipment: 2 buckets per team, a cup per player

73
Charade relay

For this relay, players sit in semi-circle groups in the corners of the hall/
room. The leader stands in the centre of the room. On the signal to
start each team sends up one person who is told a TV programme or
advertisement and this member immediately returns to his group and
tries to act it out silently in front of the group. As soon as someone
guesses it, that person runs to the leader and repeats the process. The
winning group is the first group to have acted out und guessed twenty
programmes/advertisements. The more weird and wonderful the programmes or advertisements the better.

Knowing   Communication   Drama   Bible

Equipment: None

74
Lemon twister

The simple object of this game is for each member of the team to push the lemon with the pencil along the floor in a straight line to and from a finishing line about 10 metres away.

Variation:
>   The pencil being used should be held in the
>   mouth – this creates frustration in the first degree.

Frustration   Difficulty   Bias

Equipment: Lemon and pencil per team

75
Skin the snake

Teams are formed in files. Each person in each team puts his right hand
back between his legs and his left hand forward to grasp the right hand
of the person in front. On the signal to start the last person in each
team lies back while the others move back over him until all are lying
down. Then the reverse happens.
Hilarious to watch – crazy to do!

Truth-revealed   Bible

Equipment: None

76
Mat netball

Choose two teams. This game contains all the elements of netball except shooting for goals. It is a non-contact game in which players may pass the ball, but not run with it. Goals are scored by passing the ball to a nominated player (or goalie) who stations himself on his team's goal mat. No other players are allowed on that mat – the penalty being a free goal against the infringing player's team. The game begins by tossing the ball up in the centre. There are no boundaries to the field, therefore no need for 'throw-ins'.

God – Devil

Equipment: Ball, 2 mats (or hoops)

77
Skittle ball

Choose two teams. This is a similar game to mat netball, except instead of scoring goals by passing the ball to the team goalie, the game is to throw the ball and knock down the opponents' skittle which is within their circle. Each team is allowed a goal-keeper within their circle who tries to prevent the ball hitting the skittle. No opposition players are allowed within the circle. A team scores two points each time the skittle is knocked over, and one point if the defending goalie knocks it over. Experiment with the size of the circle.

God – Devil Fellowship

Equipment: Ball, 2 skittles, 2 circles (eg hoops or chalk marks)

78
Continuous cricket

Two teams are selected. The field is marked with a base placed 3 to 5 metres to the right of the wickets, and a bowling line 5 to 7 metres in front of the wicket. Batsmen line up at the side of the playing area while the fielding team select a 'bowler' and 'backstop' and the rest spread themselves about the field. The bowler must bowl underarm and the batsmen must run around the base each time he hits the ball ('tip and run'). Besides being caught or hitting his own wickets, the batsman can only be 'out' by being bowled by the official bowler. Every time a ball is fielded it is returned to the bowler who bowls immediately. When a batsman is out, the next batsman immediately takes his place. Whilst this change is being made, the bowler may continue to bowl at the wicket. The game continues until all the players of the batting team are 'out'. The teams then change over. The team making the greater number of runs in a couple of innings is the winner.

Ensure and encourage fast movement of the ball for greatest success.

Devil Attack – offguard

Equipment: Bat, tennis ball, wickets, a base

79
Night paper tearing

Each player is given a piece of newspaper. The lights are turned out and players are instructed to tear their sheet of paper into the longest strip of paper within 4 minutes.

Take a flash picture (with announcement) to send to your local paper.

Patience – Blindness

Equipment: One sheet of newspaper per person

80
Post-mortem

A gruesome game that usually causes much amusement. The group sits in a circle in complete darkness. The leader begins to relate a murder story in extremely brutal, scarey and vivid detail (this requires good preparation and skill). At the end he indicates that the mutilated parts of the body have been found and he begins to pass these around, one at a time, for the players to feel (wait for each 'part' to make a full circuit before passing another). The following objects fulfil the purpose of the 'parts of the body'.

Brains	– A raw soggy cauliflower with the leaves trimmed off
Ear	– Dried apricot
Eyes	– Peeled grapes on their stalks
Hand	– Glove filled with wet sand
Heart	– Piece of liver
Leg	– Leg of lamb bone
Stomach	– semi-inflated balloon filled with water
Teeth	– Odd ones from the butcher or kennels
Tongue	– Raw meat
Veins	– Cold cooked macaroni
Windpipe	– Piece of soft rubber hose

If you are camping then this done late at night in one of the tents creates screams and groans that will trouble your camping neighbours.

Death – Life   God and creation

Equipment: A body!

81
Murder

The leader takes one player aside and tells her that she is to be murdered – stabbed in the back – in the course of the evening. She is coached to scream and fall when stabbed. The host also takes another player aside and coaches him/her to do the stabbing.

The one to be murdered does not know who is to do the stabbing. When the leader is ready for the event the lights are unexpectedly extinguished, a woman screams, confusion results, and after a pause long enough to allow the villain to get away from the spot the lights are turned on.

The leader immediately assembles the group, orders an investigation and insists that no one leaves the room. He asks one of the group – a distinguished and clever person – to act as the prosecuting attorney. He is not appointed until after the murder; the prosecutor's task is to discover the murderer. He quizzes each person and everyone must answer truthfully, except the murderer. Gradually as the questioning goes on, the net closes on one or two and finally the guilt of the murderer is established.

With a good prosecutor the game has limitless possibilities for entertainment. No one in the group should know that this game is to be played until the murder is committed, except of course the murderer and the victim. The victim does not know when the event is to start until the lights go out.

Naturally the victim cannot be questioned and she is encouraged to lie down in position until she is carried away or the investigation is completed.

Variation:

> Bring in a 'real' off duty detective to do the investigation to add a bit of drama and realism.

Truth   Belief

Equipment: None

82
Fashion designing

Pair off players into couples, and supply each girl with plenty of newspaper and pins. The girls have ten minutes to re-dress the male 'model' using the paper and pins (over his other clothes). Some amusing creations will emerge.

Fashion   Creation   Choice

Equipment: Large amount of newspaper and pins

83
Vocab complete

The leader begins by thinking of a word and gives the first letter. The next player thinks of a word beginning with this letter and gives the second letter. The third player thinks of a word that begins with the first two letters and gives the third letter. The object of the game is to avoid completing a word. When a player has completed three words, or fails to think of a word beginning with the letters already mentioned he is out of the game. A person can be challenged for an impossible word and if proved wrong is charged with the equivalent of completing a word.

Prayer   Guidance

84
Romantic consequences

All the players, equipped with paper and pencils, sit in a circle. The leader directs the players to write at the top of their piece of paper an adjective applicable to a girl. Papers are folded so that the writing cannot be seen and passed clock-wise to the next person. Then each person writes a girl's name on the paper, folds the paper and hands it to the next person. So the process continues till everyone writes one of each of the following on a different piece of paper:

1. An adjective applicable to a girl
2. A girl's name
3. An adjective applicable to a guy
4. A guy's name
5. Where they met.
6. What she did
7. What he did
8. What she said
9. What he said
10. The consequences
11. What the world said

Players usually try to be as clever and funny as possible; however the resulting combinations are usually quite hilarious and ludicrous. When everyone completes all the items the leader reads out the combinations by linking them in a story created from the questions.

You will appreciate that you may not be able to use this game with every group of youngsters . . . for obvious reasons.

Romanticism – Adolescence

Equipment: Sheet of paper and pencil per person

85
Creativity

Divide those present into small groups of four. Give each group a set of items, eg, an apple, matches, toothpicks, paper clips, rubber bands, cardboard, etc. Scissors and felt pens can be made available for common use.

The groups are given 20–30 minutes to create some object that would be useful in any home. They are limited in their creation to the use of the items supplied but they do have to use all of them. It should be explained that the created items will be judged on imaginativeness of purpose and efficiency of design. At the end of the 20–30 minutes of creativity each group, through a representative, must verbally 'sell' the idea to the groups. Prizes are awarded to the most imaginatively-created and best explained items. The leader must know his group well to be sure that an activity like this will work.

Creation   Design

Equipment: See paragraph 1

86
Nursery land

Players are divided into four groups, each group sitting in a different corner of the room. The object of the game is for each team to show its superior knowledge of nursery rhymes by always having one ready to sing when required. Team 1 starts by singing a nursery rhyme. When it is finished everyone joins in a chorus of the alphabet (A-Z). Then, without hesitation, team 2 must start singing its nursery rhyme and so the pattern continues. If any team cannot take their turn within 3 seconds, then it is 'out'. No nursery rhyme can be used twice.

As the leader, you will need to stand in the middle of the room and keep things going by being more extrovert than you have ever been before.

Jesus said: 'Unless you approach the Kingdom of God as a child . . . '

Faith

Equipment: None

115

Mr and Mrs

Select four couples who have been 'going together' for some time. The guys are then asked to leave the room while a set of questions is put to the girls. Ask questions like 'Where did you go for your first date?' 'What was the first thing he ever gave you? 'When it comes to spending money, what word best describes him?' The guys are then brought back and asked the same questions. Couples receive points for similar answers. This can be very good if well prepared imaginative questions and option answers are used.

Dating   Secrets

Equipment: None

88
Love letters

Divide the players into small groups, giving each group a newspaper, a pair of scissors, glue and a sheet of paper. On the signal to start each group has twenty minutes to compose a love letter choosing words and phrases from the newspaper, cutting them out and sticking them together on the sheet of paper. Results are read aloud to the group in a very romantic soppy voice.

Relationships

Equipment: Newspaper, scissors, glue and paper

89
Habit formation

Send two or three people out of the room while the rest of the group selects a habit, eg 'picking one's nose,' etc. The chosen few are then called back into the room separately and asked a number of questions by the leader and group about this habit they 'supposedly' have, eg, 'When did you first start doing it?' 'How regularly do you do it?' 'Does it ever cause any embarrassment?' 'What are the advantages of this habit?' Without knowing the habit, the person must reply to the questions by making up answers even though he does not have a clue as to what he is talking about. It usually causes much amusement, particularly if you choose imaginative characters to go out of the room.

Habits   Temptation

Equipment: None

90
Balloon debate

Five people are told that they are all in a balloon which is rapidly losing height and one of them must be thrown out. They are each given one minute to make a speech as to why they should not be the person to be thrown out. Allow three minutes for them to collect their thoughts. At the end the audience decides by vote who should be thrown out on the basis of their speeches.

Life – reasons for living Death

Equipment: None

91
'One minute please'

Leader announces a topic (something which will *cause amusement and imaginative thoughts*) and then selects at random someone who must stand and speak on the topic for one minute. If the leader does not want the blame of embarrassing anyone then use a pack of cards, the one with the Joker having to speak. Choose subjects that are going to be relevant to your study as well as amusing ones like: a bus stop; alligator wrestling; tea bags; squashed tomatoes, etc.

Expression of beliefs

Equipment; None

92
The great swanni trick

Each person writes a word or phrase on a slip of paper, folds it and puts it into a bowl. The 'mindreader' takes one of the slips from the bowl and without unfolding it, presses it against his forehead and states what is on the slip. He then asks for the writer to identify himself. An accomplice will admit to writing it. He then goes through the same process taking one slip after another.

The trick lies in the first slip which is an authentic slip, but the words on it are not the words stated by the mindreader; he states words agreed in advance with his accomplice. When the mindreader looks at the first slip for confirmation, he actually learns what is written on it. Then he holds a second slip to his forehead and pretends to state the words on it, but actually calls out the words on the first slip. He continues this technique of pretending to read the words on the slip but is actually stating the words on the preceding one. To do this properly you need to dress up in clothes that give you the magical/ mystical image.

N.B. The accomplice must only *pretend* to insert a slip of paper into the bowl at the beginning.

Magic   Deceit

Equipment: Paper, pencil, bowl

121

93
Newspaper magic

This is a trick requiring an accomplice. Nine sheets of newspaper, each with a number, are laid out on the floor in a three row by three row pattern. While the accomplice is out of the room the group chooses a numbered sheet. The accomplice returns and the leader begins to ask 'Is it this one?' After answering 'No' to the wrong choices, the accomplice answers 'Yes' to the correct numbered sheet. The trick is repeated until someone in the group works out the trick technique involved. The trick technique is very simple – the accomplice knows which sheet it is from the way the leader uses a pointer stick when asking the question. Think of every single sheet being divided into 9 sections similar to the lay-out of the nine original sheets. If the leader points to the top right hand corner of any sheet then the answer is the top sheet on the right. If the leader points to the middle of any sheet then the answer is the middle sheet in the middle row, and so on. The leader should use some imagination in his attire for this game.

Magic

Equipment: Newspaper, stick

94
Blow football

Two teams stand at opposite sides of a large table which is used as a field. Goals are marked at each end of the table with chalk and a couple of books. A ping pong ball is then placed in the centre of the table and the players begin blowing in the direction of their goals.
Variation:

> Instead of using a table use a room with everybody on all fours to ensure total chaos.

Chaos

Equipment: Table, ping-pong ball, chalk

95
Card rugby

Divide the players into two teams who are distinguished in some way. They line up on a team base line 50 metres apart. The leader stands in the centre, and suddenly throws the cards into the air and calls a particular card. All the players then dash to the centre and attempt to find the card and get it back over their base line. The game is particularly entertaining when the teams decide on using 'dummy decoy discoverers' who can lead the opposition away leaving the rest of the team time to find the right card and transfer it over the base line.

Chaos

Equipment: A very old pack of cards

96
Flour bomb torch stalk

This is an old favourite that never ceases to be the cause of great hilarity. It is especially suited to night-time conditions in a forest or sand dune area.

Two large torches are placed on two high areas 200–300 metres apart, and an area mid-way between the torches is designated United Nations territory which the leader makes his headquarters.

The players are divided into two teams and gather around their allocated torch to work out their strategy. After about fifteen minutes of strategy planning, the leader blows his whistle three times to indicate the start of the game. Half of each team then moves out to attack the opposition's torch while the other half remain to defend their torch. The simple objective is to reach the opposition's torch and turn it out. Each player is armed with flour bombs. If hit by an opposition attacker or defender the 'hit' player must report to the leader in the United Nations area.

Each team scores five points for each team member who reaches the torch, and loses one point for each member hit. Points are added up at the end of the game.

In the excitement, some team members get confused, or putting it another way – cheat! You will need to have cheat checks in the form of U.N. patrols to safeguard this activity.

War

Equipment: 2 torches, supply of flour bombs (at least 5 per player), whistle

97
Bombs away

Select six players who are divided into two teams. Each of the six players are then spaced equally apart at the edge of a circle, team members alternating. Each player is armed with five bags of flour. At the signal to start each player attempts to strike one of his opponents with a bag of flour which must burst. When struck, the player retires. The winning team is the one who can claim the last person standing without being hit. Anyone failing to throw a bag of flour for 10 seconds is disqualified.

Very messy and therefore would be a game which should be played outside.

War

Equipment: 30 paper bags filled with flour

98
Hoppob

Ideal for a group of lively teenagers. Each player stands on one leg, holding his other foot in his hand. On the signal to start players balancing on one leg hop about trying to knock other players off balance. When anyone falls or is forced to put his foot down he is disqualified. The object is to be the last player remaining.

Aggression   Balance

Equipment: None

99
Snail – cycling

Each player rides his bicycle over a specified course. The object is to be the last to finish. If a player puts a foot to the ground he is disqualified.

Life – Purpose of   pace of   aim of

100
Water jousting

Have a narrow plank stretched across a stream or mounted on a triangular stand. Two players equipped with pillows straddle the plank and attempt to knock each other off the plank into the water.

Why not have a knock-out competition!

Ambition   Failure

Equipment: Plank, 2 pillows

101
Three legged soccer

Tie pairs of player's legs as for a three legged race. Divide the pairs into teams, establish a set of goals at either end of a small field and play soccer as normal.
Variation:
>   Four-legged soccer (tying 3 pairs of legs together)

Teamwork   Fellowship

Equipment: Ball, material for tying legs

102
Egg throwing competition

Couples stand one pace apart and toss a raw egg to each other. They step back one pace each toss. The winning couple is the one which is the furthest apart and keeps their egg intact. Some efforts result in most amusing sticky ends.

Abilities

Equipment: One egg per couple

103
Slimy tug–o–war

Create a large 'mud patch' as the central point in a tug–of–war. Make sure you have plenty of mud by leaving a hose running.

Temptation – the result of giving in   Sinning – dragging you in

Equipment: Old rope, mud patch

104
Crab football

Establish two goal lines. Divide the players into two teams and have them sit on the goal lines facing each other with arms extended backwards supporting the body from the ground. Place a large rubber ball on the ground mid-way between the goals. At the signal both teams move toward the ball, keeping the crab position, and attempt to kick the ball over the opposing goal line. They can kick it with one foot or drop it and kick it with both feet. Players cannot stand up or touch the ball with their hands.

Variation

1 After the game has been played for a while, substitute a balloon for the ball. After being accustomed to the ball, the slow moving balloon causes much amusement.

2 Use a rugger ball

Life as it is and not how it should be

Equipment: Large rubber ball

105
Back–to–back race

A team is made up of two players who stand back to back with their arms linked. On the signal to start they run towards a line, one running forwards, the other backwards. As soon as they touch the line they start back, reversing positions.

Variation:

1 Ask the players to try this sideways.

2 Ask the players to start by getting up from the floor in their back to back positions

Partnership   Relationships

Equipment: None

106
Broom twist

Divide the group into two teams. Place a broom in front of each team. At the given signal each team member in turn must pick up the broom, hold the end close to his chest, and *looking up* at the brush twist it 15 times as fast as he can. The winning team, if there is one still standing, is the one who completes the assignment. It is essential that each team member looks up and is encouraged to go as fast as they can. Also important is the necessity to have someone to count the twists (as the player may not be in a fit position to do so) and be prepared to catch the player if he feels he wants to drop out!

Confusion   Unbalanced

Equipment: 2 brooms

107
Scissors

Ask the group to sit on the floor in a circle and pass the scissors around. Each person has to say whether the scissors are 'crossed' or 'not crossed' when they pass them on irrespective of whether they are 'crossed' (open) or 'not crossed' (closed). When they pass them on they may or may not be correct, eg, they may pass them on 'crossed' but may say 'not crossed' and may be correct or vice versa.

The secret of the game is not whether the scissors are crossed at all but whether the legs of the person who is speaking are 'crossed' or 'not crossed'.

There is much amusement and frustration as people try to puzzle out how some people are correct and some are not even though there appears to be no scissor pattern at all.

Knowing   Embarrassment

Equipment: Scissors

108
This is a . . .

Ask the group to sit in a circle and pass any object to the person on their left, eg, a pen or pencil. You say as you are passing it: 'This is a . . .' and then you describe it perhaps as a 'jug'. The person on your left then must pass it on and describe it in a different way. However some people will describe it 'correctly', even though they will all be different while others will not.

The secret of this one is that whatever description you may give to the pencil must start with the first letter of the name of the person on your left; eg, I could use 'jug' if the name of the person on my left was Jill, Jim or Janet.

As the article returns to you, you change the description each time eg, 'jacket' causing even more frustration and curiosity among those who have not found the solution.

Problem solving

Equipment: None

109
Marshmallow stuff

Ask for 3 volunteers and yet at the same time volunteer 3 that would be suitable for such a game. Have the three blindfolded and sat on chairs with a packet of marshmallows each. Tell them that it's a competition and that the winner is the one who can eat the most in 3 minutes. Arrange for three others to do the counting and someone to do the time-check.

Give the signal to go and encourage loud shouts for each of the contestants. However after about 15 seconds quietly take the blindfolds off two of them, telling them to go back to their places leaving just one person stuffing their face. As your audience are still shouting for all three (you keep pointing to the empty chairs) the unfortunate person left still thinks he is in competition.

After about 2 minutes, signal to the audience to stop as you remove the blindfold. Get someone to take a picture the moment the victim realises what has happened. Absolutely fantastic game on deceit. This is perhaps one of the cruellest and nastiest games in the book, giving it my award for one of the best in the book.

Deceit   Gluttony

Equipment: 3 bags of marshmallows, 3 blindfolds, 3 chairs

110
Voluntary fear

This is probably at its best when played after a nasty game; it is not a dance, in fact it's setting a situation to do nothing.

Ask for two volunteers and send them out of the room. Tell the rest that when you call in the volunteers nothing at all is going to happen; you are just going to ask them to sit down in their places and that you are going to carry on as if nothing has happened. Also ask your group to say nothing if they are asked anything by the volunteers.

The unknown, the fear of what might happen makes the volunteers very uneasy and therefore makes an excellent starter later on during the course of your activities to discuss fear, using the volunteers as examples.

Fear   The Unknown   Void

Equipment: None

Alphabetical Index

Index of Subjects

Kind of Crowdbreaker

Crowdbreakers that can be used outdoors:
5; 26; 27; 34; 40; 41; 42; 46; 52; 54; 58; 59; 61; 65; 66; 67; 68; 69; 71; 72; 73; 75; 76;77; 78; 95; 96; 97; 98; 99; 100; 101; 102; 103; 104; 106

Good Starters:
1; 2; 3; 4; 6; 8; 11; 23; 67

Musical Crowdbreakers:
4; 7; 9; 22; 68; 86

Pencil and Paper Crowdbreakers:
1; 2; 3; 4; 12; 84; 92

Boisterous Crowdbreakers:
5; 8; 13; 15; 17; 19; 20; 21; 24; 25; 26; 27; 29; 30; 34; 65; 67; 94; 97; 98; 100; 104; 106

Crowdbreakers Suitable for Adults:
1; 2; 3; 4; 7; 11; 12; 22; 23; 30; 31; 32; 33; 44; 45; 50; 52; 68; 69; 71; 73; 79; 82; 83; 87; 91; 92; 94; 107; 108; 109

Crowdbreakers Needing No Equipment:
5; 11; 20; 21; 24; 38; 58; 67; 73; 75; 81; 83; 87; 89; 90; 91; 110

Team Crowdbreakers:
8; 15; 16; 17; 18; 19; 20; 27; 29; 30; 34; 35; 38; 61; 62; 63; 64; 65; 67; 68; 69; 70; 71; 75; 76; 77; 78; 85; 86; 88; 94; 95; 96; 97; 101; 103; 104; 106

Partner Crowdbreakers:
12; 23; 33; 37; 39; 40; 42; 43; 44; 50; 51; 52; 53; 54; 66; 82; 87; 102